I0800869

WonderWorks

Decodable Reader

Unit 5

McGraw Hill

Contents

It Can Spin
by Anita Monroe
Illustrated by Beth Mills
1

Sid Can Hop
by Celine Robbins
9

My Pet Ed
by Albert Santiago
illustrated by Kate Flanagan
17

It Can Spin

by Anita Monroe

Illustrated by Beth Mills

Tom can spin **the** top.
Stan can spin the top.

Stan can snap the  .

top

Do **you** see it **go**?
It can spin!

Can Tom stop the top?
Can Stan stop it?

The top did not stop.

Can a cat stop it?
It can!

Sid Can Hop

Lori Adamski Peek/Workbook Stock/Getty Images

by Celine Robbins

Cappi Thompson/Flickr/Getty Images

A  can sit.
dog

It can sit, sit, sit.

Christian Rummel/iStock/Getty Images

A bat can nap.
It can nap, nap, nap.

GK Hart/Vikki Hart/Taxi/Getty Images

A cat can tip it.
It can tip, tip, tip it.

Cappi Thompson/Flickr/Getty Images

A  can tap.
bird

It can tap, tap, tap.

Rubberball/Mike Kemp/Getty Images

My tan  can hop.

rabbit

See him hop, hop, hop.

I like **my** Sid!

My Pet Ed

by Albert Santiago
illustrated by Kate Flanagan

ED

I am Ted.

I like  .

dogs

Mom set Ed on the  .

grass

Ted met Ed.

Ted ran.
Ed ran.

Ed ran, ran, ran.
Ted ran, ran, ran.

Ted and Ed sat on a  .

bike

Ted can pet Ed.
Ted and Ed **are**  !
friends

Unit 5

Word Count: 41

Decodable Words

Target Phonics Element: *s*-Blends
snap, spin, Stan, stop
Review: *can, cat, did, it, not, Tom, top*

High-Frequency Words

and, do, go, you
Review: *a, and, see, the*

Word Count: 52

Decodable Words

Target Phonics Element: Consonant /h/*h*
him, hop
Review: *bat, can, cat, it, nap, Sid, sit, tan, tap, tip*

High-Frequency Words

my
Review: *a, I, like, see*

Week 3 • *My Pet Ed*

Word Count: 41

Decodable Words

Target Phonics Element: Short *e*

Ed, met, pet, set, Ted

Review: *am, can, Mom, on, ran, sat*

High-Frequency Words

are

Review: *a, and, I, like, my*

Decoding skills taught to date:

Consonants /m/*m*, /s/s, /p/*p*, /t/*t*; Short *a*; Short *i*; Initial and Final /n/*n*; Initial /k/*c*; Short *o*; Initial and Final /d/*d*; Consonant /h/*h*; Short *e*; Blends *sn, sp, st*